Akua Hawai'i

Hawaiian Gods and Their Stories

written by Kimo Armitage

illustrations by Solomon Enos

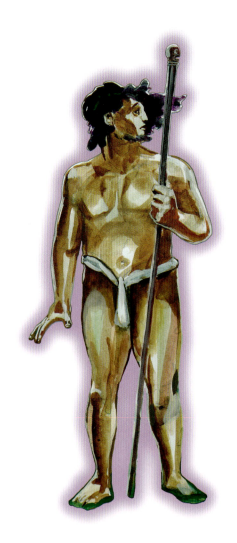

For my sister, Cathrine.
—Kimo Armitage

Thank you to the people who have contributed their manaʻo to these illustrations of Hawaiian akua. I would especially like to thank the Hui at Hale Noa.
—Solomon Enos

Copyright © 2005 by Bishop Museum
Copyright © 2005 text by Kimo Armitage
1525 Bernice Street
Honolulu, Hawaiʻi 96817
www.bishopmuseum.org/press

All Rights Reserved.

No portion of this book may be reproduced in whole or in part, in any form or by any means, electronic or mechanical, including photocopying, or by any information storage and retrieval system now known or hereafter invented, without prior written permission from the Bishop Museum Press.

ISBN 1-58178-042-7

Design by Gary N. Nomura

Printed in Korea

Library of Congress Cataloging-in-Publication Data
Armitage, Kimo. Akua Hawaiʻi: Hawaiian gods and their stories
by Kimo Armitage; illustrated by Solomon Enos. p. cm.
Includes bibliographical references.
ISBN 1-58178-042-7 (hardcover : alk. paper)
1. Hawaiian mythology--Juvenile literature.
I. Enos, Solomon, ill. II. Title.
BL2620.H3A76 2005
299'.9242--dc22

Contents

Introduction

Pō

Kumulipo and Pōʻele

Papahānaumoku & Wākea

Hoʻohōkūkalani, Hāloanakalaukapalili, & Hāloa

Kāne, Kanaloa, Kū, & Lono

Haumea

Nāmakaokahaʻi & Pelehonuamea

Hiʻiakaikapoliopele

Kamohoaliʻi & Nanaue

Kaʻahupahau & Kahiʻukā

Kamapuaʻa

Poliʻahu

Lilinoe, Waiau, & Kahoupokāne

Keaomelemele

Moʻoinanea

Kūʻulakai & Hinapukuiʻa

ʻAiʻaikūʻulakai

Sources

I ka wā kahiko, strong, handsome people came from across the vast ocean in splendid canoes to Hawai'i.

They brought with them their foods, their customs, their language, and their gods. Their gods are the phenomenal spectacles of the natural environment – fresh water, thunder, clouds, and volcanic eruptions.

Many Hawaiian gods are superhuman and live in Nuʻumealani or Kuaihelani. Many gods dwell with Hawaiians. Humble mortals invoke the gods' names to call upon their wondrous abilities for help and guidance.

The moʻolelo of the gods are branded upon many sacred places where the gods perform their glorious feats. To earn their favor was to be victorious in battle or successful in harvest. To incur their wrath meant severe hardship.

Many of the gods are noble creatures: the wild boar, the shark, the porpoise, and the multi-hued corals. Since most of them have multiple forms, they are able to dwell anywhere in the many different regions that combine to form the Hawaiian archipelago.

Hawaiians worship the male and female aspects of nature and its diverse incarnations. The union of male and female brings forth new life.

Pō

Time begins with darkness. Her name is Pō.

O ke au i kahuli wela ka honua
  At that time that turned the heat of the earth,

O ke au i kahuli lole ka lani
  At the time when the heavens turned and changed,

O ke au i kūkaʻiaka ka lā
  At the time when the light of the sun was subdued

E hoʻomālamalama i ka mālama
  To cause light to break forth,

O ke au o Makaliʻi ka pō
  At the time of the night of Makaliʻi (winter)

O ka walewale hoʻokumu honua ia
  Then began the slime which established the earth,

O ke kumu o ka lipo, i lipo ai
  The source of deepest darkness

O ke kumu o ka Pō, i pō ai.
  The source of deepest night.

O ka lipolipo, o ka lipolipo,
   Of the depth of darkness, of the depth of darkness,

O ka lipo o ka lā, 'o ka lipo o ka pō,
   Of the darkness of the sun, in the depth of night,

Pō wale hō'i.
   It is night.

— **Kumulipo,**
Translation by Queen Lili'uokalani, 1895

Pō is the night. Pō is the darkness. She is the first to come forth.
                              Everything begins with her.

Kumulipo & Pō'ele

Pō gives birth to two children, a son named Kumulipo and a daughter named Pōʻele. Through their union, Kumulipo and Pōʻele create the natural world. All children born to them are gods.

The first god-child born to Kumulipo and Pōʻele is the ʻākoʻakoʻa, the coral polyp. The coral polyp creates a foundation in the sea.

From darkness came life.

Papahānaumoku & Wākea

Papahānaumoku and Wākea are among the descendants of Pō. Papahānaumoku is a glorious woman, and she attracts the attention of Wākea, a magnificent man.

Papahānaumoku means "Papa who gives birth to islands," a name she aptly deserves because the first child born from her union with Wākea is the island of Hawai'i.

Papahānaumoku and Wākea are inseparable, and they spend entire days and nights together. Soon the next child born to them is Maui, who is followed by Kaho'olawe. Kaho'olawe is also known as Kanaloa because he is born in the shape of a porpoise.

Although Papahānaumoku and Wākea are still married and love each other deeply, Papahānaumoku one day decides to travel to Kapakapakaua, a place in Tahiti. A lonely Wākea seeks the comfort of another woman and meets the beautiful Ka'ula. Ka'ula and Wākea have a child whom they name Lāna'ika'ula, a red island.

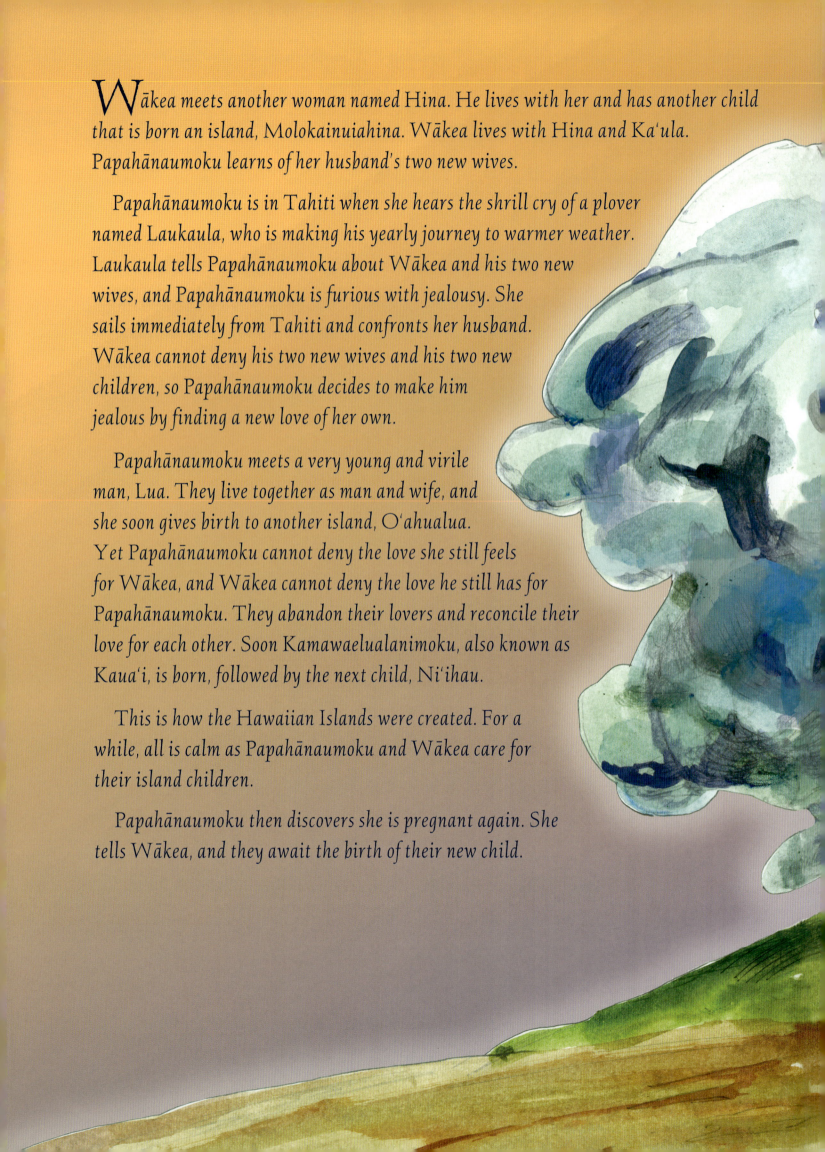

Wākea meets another woman named Hina. He lives with her and has another child that is born an island, Molokainuiahina. Wākea lives with Hina and Ka'ula. Papahānaumoku learns of her husband's two new wives.

Papahānaumoku is in Tahiti when she hears the shrill cry of a plover named Laukaula, who is making his yearly journey to warmer weather. Laukaula tells Papahānaumoku about Wākea and his two new wives, and Papahānaumoku is furious with jealousy. She sails immediately from Tahiti and confronts her husband. Wākea cannot deny his two new wives and his two new children, so Papahānaumoku decides to make him jealous by finding a new love of her own.

Papahānaumoku meets a very young and virile man, Lua. They live together as man and wife, and she soon gives birth to another island, O'ahualua. Yet Papahānaumoku cannot deny the love she still feels for Wākea, and Wākea cannot deny the love he still has for Papahānaumoku. They abandon their lovers and reconcile their love for each other. Soon Kamawaelualanimoku, also known as Kaua'i, is born, followed by the next child, Ni'ihau.

This is how the Hawaiian Islands were created. For a while, all is calm as Papahānaumoku and Wākea care for their island children.

Papahānaumoku then discovers she is pregnant again. She tells Wākea, and they await the birth of their new child.

Hoʻohōkūkalani, Hāloanakalaukapalili, & Hāloa

Hoʻohōkūkalani is the daughter of Papahānaumoku and Wākea. When she is born, Wākea takes her into his arms, marvels at this most beautiful daughter, and loves her unconditionally.

As Hoʻohōkūkalani matures into a stunning, young woman, Wākea finds himself falling in love with her. His only thoughts are of spending time alone with her, which is impossible because Papahānaumoku is always present. Wākea consults his priest, Komoʻawa, as to how Wākea can be alone with Hoʻohōkūkalani.

Komoʻawa instructs Wākea to tell Papahānaumoku that, from this moment on, only men will do the cooking and only men will eat certain foods. Wākea must also tell Papahānaumoku that when she has her menses, she must wait in the Hale Peʻa until her bleeding stops. The restriction on the food she may and may not eat is called the ʻaikapu. Papahānaumoku agrees to her husband's commands, and when it is her time to stay at the Hale Peʻa, Wākea is able to be alone with Hoʻohōkūkalani.

When Papahānaumoku finds out that Wākea has cheated on her again, she is angry. She bids goodbye to her children and leaves for Tahiti, never to return.

Hoʻohōkūkalani becomes pregnant, but delivers a stillborn child. She is inconsolable. She holds her dead son in her arms and refuses to let him go. Hoʻohōkūkalani and Wākea mourn for their dead child. They decide to bury their son in the soil behind their house, and they name the boy Hāloanakalaukapalili.

Soon after Hoʻohōkūkalani and Wākea bury their son, they notice that a plant begins to grow from his grave. This plant is the taro. Hoʻohōkūkalani continues to mourn the death of her son until she discovers she is expecting again.

This time, she gives birth to a healthy son. Hoʻohōkūkalani and Wākea name this son Hāloa, after his older brother Hāloanakalaukapalili. Because the younger Hāloa cultivates the taro and takes care of the islands, an important relationship develops. The taro and the land take care of Hāloa by providing food, and in turn, Hāloa takes care of the taro and the land; the younger brother takes care of the elder brothers, and the elder brothers take care of the younger brother. This relationship has endured until this day because the Hawaiian people are descendants of Hāloa.

Kāne

Kāne is the god of procreation, and the ancestor of chiefs and commoners.

Among the body forms of Kāne are taro, fresh water, sugar cane, ti leaf, ginger, and bamboo.

Kāne is frequently connected to freshwater streams, freshwater springs, fishponds, and ʻawa drinking. He is also known for the cultivation of plants. Breadfruit, ʻawa, and the mulberry plants are sacred to Kāne.

Kanaloa

Kanaloa is the Hawaiian god of the ocean, sailing, and ocean voyaging.

Among the body forms of Kanaloa are banana, octopus, and porpoise.

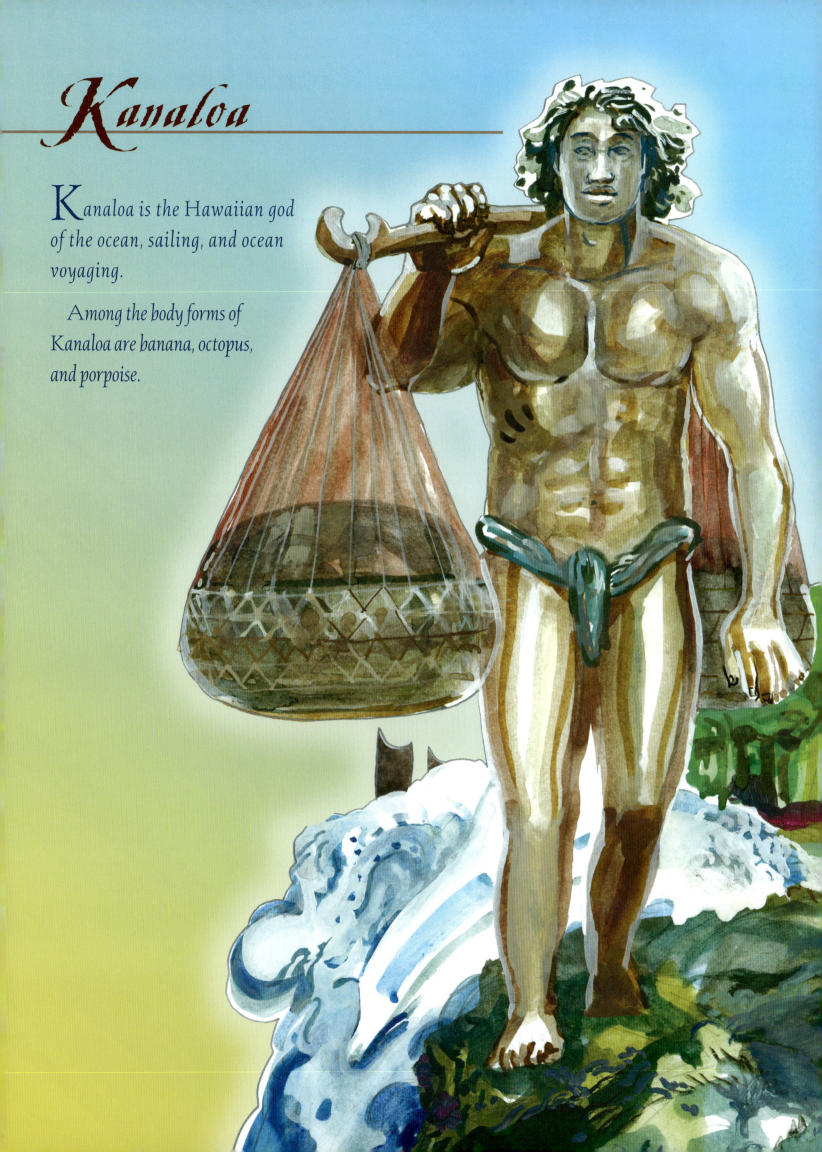

Kū

Kū is the god of war and agriculture, the forest and rain, canoes, husbandry, and fishing.

Among the body forms of Kū are coconut, breadfruit, ʻōhiʻa lehua, caterpillars, worms, and sea cucumbers.

Lono

Lono is the Hawaiian god of agricultural fertility, medicine, and peace.

Among the body forms of Lono are gourds, rain clouds, sweet potato, and pigs.

Lono is also the god of the Makahiki, a period of four months in which war and labor are forbidden and Hawaiians enjoy feasting and games.

Haumea

Haumea is the great goddess associated with childbirth. Hawaiian women pray to Haumea to ease their birthing pains. She is the worshipped ancestress of gods, goddesses, chiefs, and commoners.

Haumea is also known for the many ways in which she has given birth to her wondrous children:

    Kamohoaliʻi, a shark god, is born from the top of Haumea's head.
    Kānehekili, the god of thunder, is born from her mouth.
    Kauilanuimākāhāikalani, the god of lightning, is born from her eyes.
    Kūhaimoana, a shark god, is born from her ears.
    Kānemilohaʻi, the soul-catching god, is born from her right palm.
    Leho, a fishing god, is born from her knuckles.
    Kāneikōkala, a shark god who saves the shipwrecked and brings them safely to shore, is born from her fingers.
    Nāmakaokahaʻi, goddess of the ocean, is born from her breasts.
    Pelehonuamea, goddess of the volcano, is born from her thighs.
    Kapōʻulakīnaʻu, goddess who restores life and brings death.
    Kapōkohelele, goddess who restores life and brings death.
    Hiʻiakakalukalu, a goddess of vegetation, is born from her toes.
    Hiʻiakakuilei, a goddess of vegetation, is born from her feet.
    Hiʻiakaikapoliopele, a goddess of vegetation and healing, is born from her left palm in the shape of an egg.

Haumea also possesses selected trees that are used to sculpt war idols. Men pray to these gods for favor in war and politics. A section of Haumea's body is whittled into the female goddess Makalei, who attracts fish. But Haumea's greatest power is her ability to forever appear young. It is with this power that she emerges through consecutive generations, enriching the mana of her family line by bearing high-ranking offspring.

Nāmakaokahaʻi & Pelehonuamea

Nāmakaokahaʻi, the daughter of Haumea, is born from the breast of Haumea. She is the powerful goddess of the ocean. The waves and ocean currents respond to her command.

Pelehonuamea is the daughter of Haumea. Pelehonuamea is the great goddess of volcanoes. Her temper burns hot in the form of lava flows covering the mountainside.

When Pelehonuamea is born, she and her sister Nāmakaokahaʻi immediately begin to fight. Their confrontation is the titanic clash between ocean and lava that can still be seen today. Haumea fears for Pelehonuamea's life because Haumea knows that Pelehonuamea's fires are no match for the cold ocean waters of Nāmakaokahaʻi. Haumea gives Pelehonuamea a canoe and orders her to find another home far away from Nāmakaokahaʻi.

Pelehonuamea asks her brother Kamohoaliʻi, a shark, to guide her canoe to faraway lands. They load the canoe with provisions, and as she is about to leave, Haumea gives Pelehonuamea an egg, which she places in her bosom for safekeeping. A sister is soon born from this egg, and she is named Hiʻiakaikapoliopele, Hiʻiaka in the bosom of Pelehonuamea. She becomes Pelehonuamea's most favorite sister and closest confidant.

Nāmakaokahaʻi relentlessly chases Pelehonuamea across the wide expanse of the Pacific Ocean, and each time Pelehonuamea finds land, Nāmakaokahaʻi extinguishes Pelehonuamea's sacred fires with her ocean waves.

Pelehonuamea and her companions sail to the Northwestern Hawaiian Islands and atolls, but Nāmakaokahaʻi continues to thwart Pelehonuamea.

Pelehonuamea travels south from the Northwestern Hawaiian Islands where she lands on the island of Niʻihau. Again, Nāmakaokahaʻi finds her and extinguishes her fires. From island to island, the sisters do battle and Nāmakaokahaʻi is always victorious.

Kamohoaliʻi guides Pelehonuamea's canoe to the island of Maui where Pelehonuamea believes she is safe. The island is so high, she is certain that Nāmakaokahaʻi cannot possibly reach her, but she is mistaken.

Nāmakaokahaʻi finds Pelehonuamea and pummels her with wave after wave. The last wave, which is the strongest, traps Pelehonuamea and slams her body onto the ground, breaking every bone in her body. The place on Maui where the physical body of Pelehonuamea is destroyed is named Kaʻiwiopele, the bones of Pele.

Since Pelehonuamea is free from her physical form, she is able to travel faster, and she reaches Kīlauea on the island of Hawaiʻi. Kīlauea is so high, Nāmakaokahaʻi is unable to reach Pelehonuamea. Pelehonuamea finds a home at last.

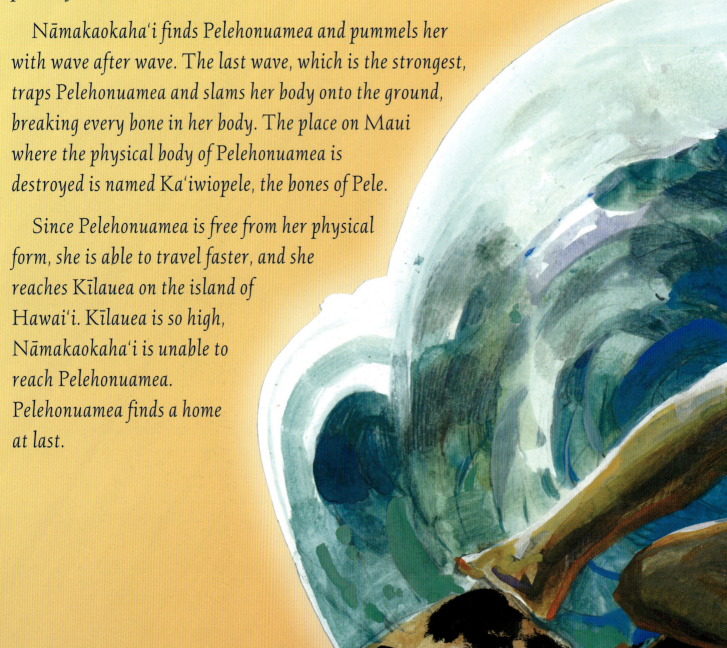

Hiʻiakaikapoliopele

Hiʻiakaikapoliopele is Pelehonuamea's youngest sister and her closest confidant. One day, Pelehonuamea tells her sisters, who live with her on the summit of Kīlauea, that she would like to sleep and under no circumstances is she to be awakened; however, if Pelehonuamea must tend to an urgent matter, only her favorite sister Hiʻiakaikapoliopele may wake her.

Pelehonuamea sleeps for several days. Soon the sisters become frightened and want to wake her, but they also fear their older sister, so they pay heed to her instructions.

While Pelehonuamea is sleeping, her spirit leaves her body and is drawn to the sound of chanting and merriment on the island of Kauaʻi.

When Pelehonuamea nears the source of the chanting, she is immediately attracted to a handsome Hawaiian chief named Lohiauipo. Lohiauipo returns the attention.

For several days, Pelehonuamea and Lohiauipo enjoy each other's company, while Hiʻiakaikapoliopele dances in the pandanus groves of Puna with her companion Hōpoe.

After many nights together, Pelehonuamea tells Lohiauipo that she must return to her homeland. Lohiauipo is heartbroken, but Pelehonuamea tells him that she will send someone to bring him to her, and then she disappears into the ocean.

When Pelehonuamea awakens from her spirit-traveling sleep, she summons all of her sisters and tells them about her adventures and her new love, Lohiauipo. She asks her sisters if one of them could travel to Kauaʻi and bring Lohiauipo back to her. All the sisters decline. They are afraid of the long journey and the numerous moʻo, lizard-like water creatures who can take the form of humans.

Only the very young, inexperienced, and devoted Hiʻiakaikapoliopele agrees to make this journey. She does so only with Pelehonuamea's promise to guard her beloved forest of lehua trees and her companion Hōpoe.

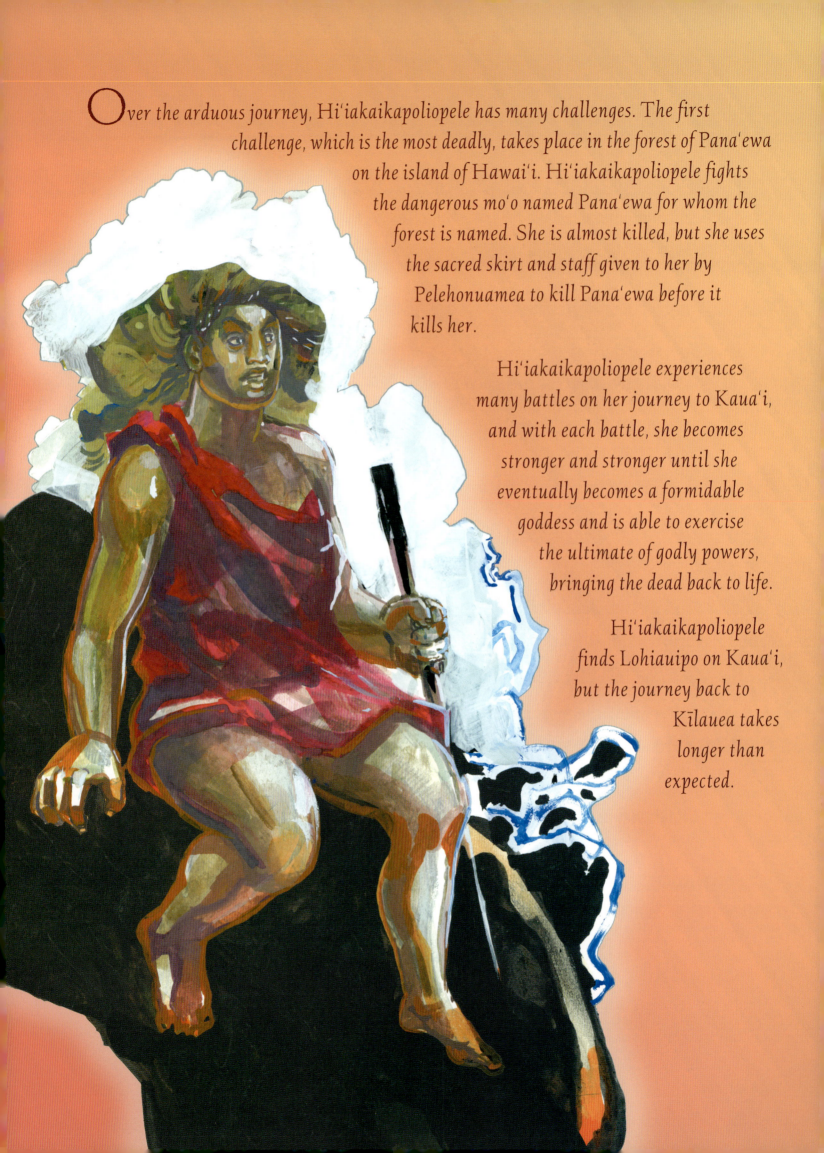

Over the arduous journey, Hiʻiakaikapoliopele has many challenges. The first challenge, which is the most deadly, takes place in the forest of Panaʻewa on the island of Hawaiʻi. Hiʻiakaikapoliopele fights the dangerous moʻo named Panaʻewa for whom the forest is named. She is almost killed, but she uses the sacred skirt and staff given to her by Pelehonuamea to kill Panaʻewa before it kills her.

Hiʻiakaikapoliopele experiences many battles on her journey to Kauaʻi, and with each battle, she becomes stronger and stronger until she eventually becomes a formidable goddess and is able to exercise the ultimate of godly powers, bringing the dead back to life.

Hiʻiakaikapoliopele finds Lohiauipo on Kauaʻi, but the journey back to Kīlauea takes longer than expected.

When Hiʻiakaikapoliopele finally returns to Kīlauea, she discovers her impatient sister has burned her beloved lehua groves to the ground and killed Hōpoe. Hiʻiakaikapoliopele vows revenge. She digs a hole to connect the ocean to Pelehonuamea's sacred fires. Her plan – to extinguish her sister as her sister has extinguished the life of the fragile Hōpoe.

The pantheons of gods intervene, realizing that should either sister die, her death would wreak havoc on the natural order of life and growth. The gods order a truce, and the sisters agree.

After the volcanoes of Pelehonuamea create new land, among the first plants to grow are the beloved lehua tree and ferns of Hiʻiakaikapoliopele. The creation of new land is followed by the growth of new vegetation. These sister-gods ensure that the life of the land continues.

Kamohoali'i & Nanaue

Kamohoali'i is the supreme shark god and the eldest son of Haumea. Kamohoali'i has the ability to change his body into many forms such as a human, a mo'o, a wrasse, or an owl. Fishermen plead to Kamohoali'i in his shark form to chase fish towards the shore, making them easier to catch.

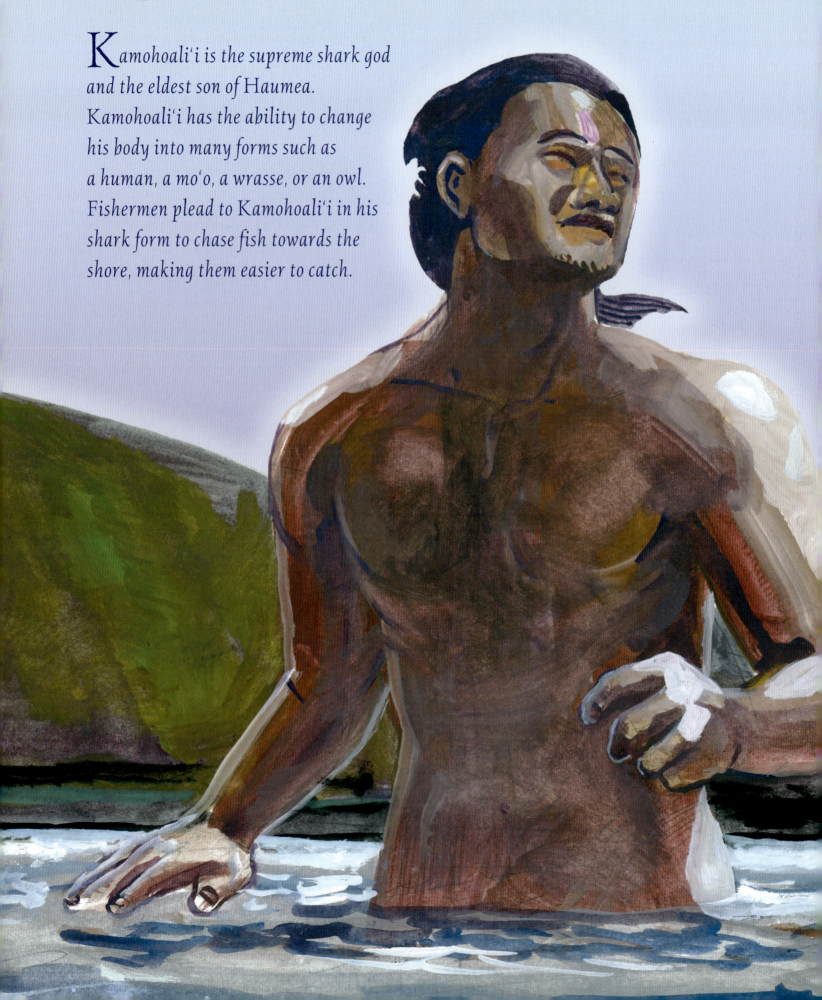

When he is not in the ocean, the home of Kamohoaliʻi is on a steep precipice overlooking Kīlauea crater. His home is so sacred that even Pelehonuamea would not dare to allow smoke to blow across its path.

One day when Kamohoaliʻi is in his shark form, he tours the waters surrounding the island of Hawaiʻi and wanders into the mouth of the Waipiʻo River, where he catches sight of a beautiful Hawaiian woman named Kalei. Kamohoaliʻi changes into a man and walks up to Kalei. She is immediately awestruck by the handsome and nude Kamohoaliʻi. They live together for a while as man and wife, but Kamohoaliʻi cannot deny his longing for the ocean, and in time, he decides he must leave Kalei.

Before Kamohoaliʻi departs, he tells Kalei that she is expecting a male child, and that she must not, under any circumstances, feed their son any variety of meat. Kamohoaliʻi leaves a red cape for his unborn son and jumps into the sea.

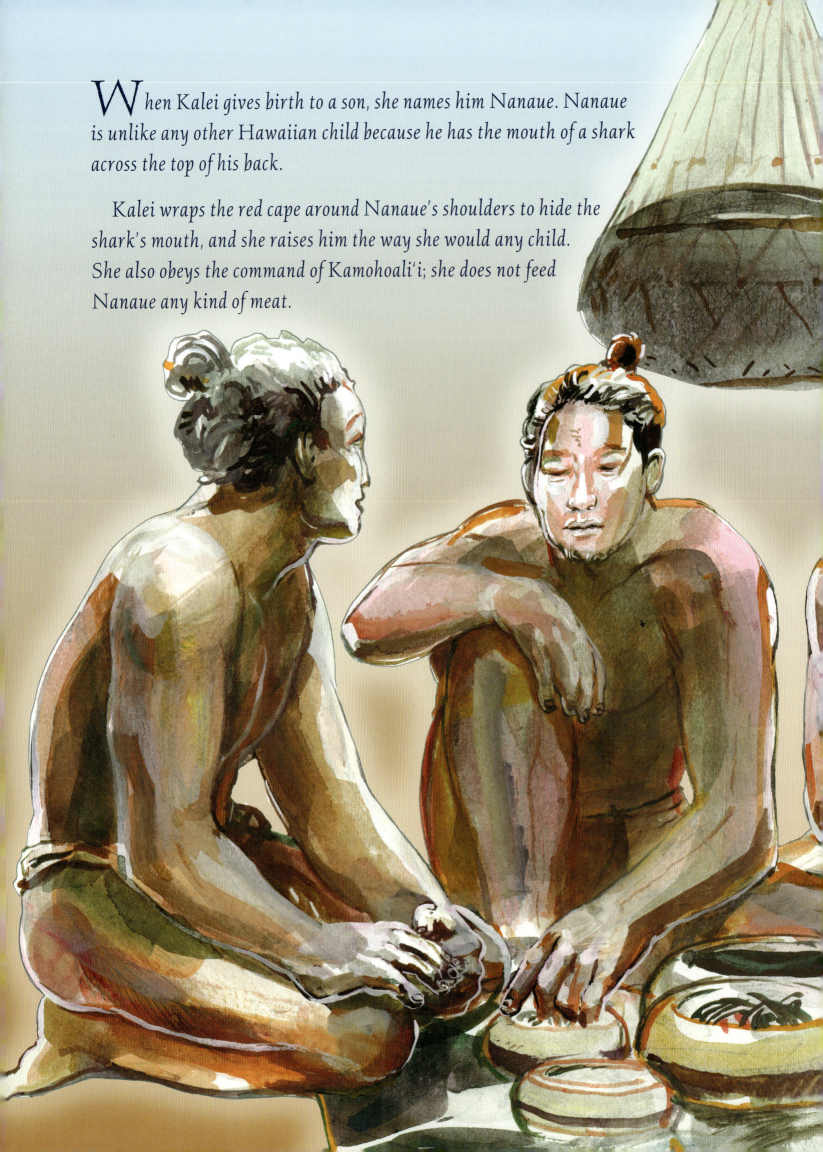

When Kalei gives birth to a son, she names him Nanaue. Nanaue is unlike any other Hawaiian child because he has the mouth of a shark across the top of his back.

Kalei wraps the red cape around Nanaue's shoulders to hide the shark's mouth, and she raises him the way she would any child. She also obeys the command of Kamohoaliʻi; she does not feed Nanaue any kind of meat.

When Nanaue is old enough to take his meals in the men's eating house, Kalei is unable to supervise the kinds of food he eats, and Kalei's father, not knowing of the restriction that had been placed on Nanaue, feeds pork to the boy.

Nanaue becomes ravenous for more meat and consumes all the meat he can find. Eventually, Nanaue turns to eating human flesh.

To satisfy his irrepressible appetite for human flesh, Nanaue begins to stalk swimmers. He waits until he finds someone alone in the water and then quickly devours his victim. Soon there is talk amongst the villagers. "There is a man-eating shark lurking in the water! Avoid swimming alone!" Kalei hears these warnings, and she suspects that Nanaue is the man-eating shark, but her love for her son overpowers her anguish.

Nanaue begins to ask villagers if they are going swimming, and when they naively reply "yes," he races to the ocean, changes into a shark, and waits for his victims. Nanaue cannot control his desire for human flesh, and he continues to eat innocent victims for many years.

One hot day, as the men of the village are working in the taro patch, a friend pulls Nanaue's red cape from his shoulders, revealing the large, gaping shark's mouth and his guilt.

The men chase Nanaue with spears, but he is too fast for them. He reaches the water, jumps in, turns into a shark, and disappears.

Nanaue escapes to Hāna where he meets and then marries a woman. And although it seems as if he is living a content life, he still cannot overcome his need for human flesh. Nanaue begins to eat villagers until he is found out and chased off.

This time Nanaue escapes to the island of Moloka'i, but the people of Moloka'i already have been warned about the infamous man-eating shark that travels from island to island eating swimmers. The people of Moloka'i capture Nanaue and his body is butchered and then burned.

Nanaue's story is a tragic one. If the command of Kamohoali'i had been obeyed and respected, his son Nanaue would have lived a life without torment.

Ka'ahupāhau & Kahi'ukā

Ka'ahupāhau and her brother Kahi'ukā are the guardian shark gods of Pu'uloa in 'Ewa, O'ahu. They protect fishermen who depend on the fertile waters for food by defending them from man-eating sharks. Hawaiian families revere these two shark gods and show their appreciation by bringing them food and 'awa. When fishermen catch fish, Ka'ahupāhau and Kahi'ukā are given the first of the catch. Hawaiians also keep the guardian shark gods clean by scraping barnacles off their bodies.

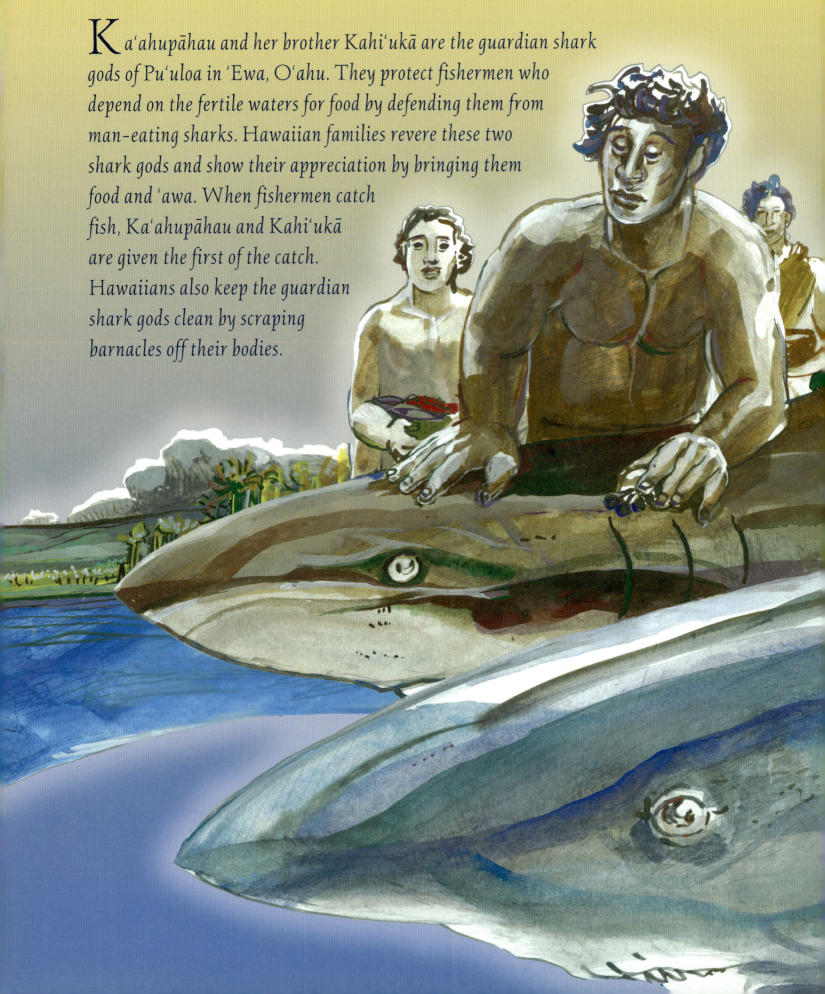

Kaʻahupāhau resides in waters off of Honouliuli. Kahiʻukā lives in the waters of Mokuʻumeʻume. Together they patrol the area, and in turn, are worshipped and cared for by the Hawaiian people.

Kamapuaʻa

Kamapuaʻa is the adventurous, wandering son of Hina and the grandson of the spectacular seer Kamaununiho. Kamapuaʻa has the ability to change into many forms, and he uses this ability to his benefit.

In one of his many adventures, Kamapuaʻa changes into the form of a gigantic pig and stretches his body like a bridge to help his family escape the guards of the stingy chief, ʻOlopana. ʻOlopana hoards food while the people of his district starve, and Kamapuaʻa finds this unacceptable. After a grueling battle with ʻOlopana's men, Kamapuaʻa slays ʻOlopana and his army.

It is in the form of a handsome Hawaiian man that Kamapuaʻa challenges and prevails over the anger of the goddess Pelehonuamea. She becomes attracted to him and takes him as her lover after a glorious battle. And it is in his many plant forms – such as the kāwaʻu, ʻōhiʻahā, ʻahakea, hao, ʻaiea, olomea, ʻamaʻu, and the ʻiʻiʻi – that he is able to alter Pelehonuamea's barren volcanic landscape into a lush forest.

Kamapuaʻa is also able to change into the humuhumunukunukuāpuaʻa, a fish. In the form of this fish, he is able to travel from island to island by swimming across the different Hawaiian channels.

Kamapuaʻa also has the ability to perform the highest feat accorded to a Hawaiian god: He is able to bring a dead person back to life. He performs the stringent rites and ceremonies to successfully bring his brother Kekeleiʻaikū back to life.

Poliʻahu

Poliʻahu is the exquisite snow goddess of Mauna Kea. In spite of her extraordinary beauty, she is destined never to win in the war of love.

One day as ʻAiwohikūpua, a young chief from Kauaʻi, is touring the area of Hāna on the island of Maui, he meets a beautiful chiefess, Hinaikamālama, who is surfing. Hinaikamālama sees ʻAiwohikūpua as well and falls desperately in love with him.

They play a friendly game of kōnane to test each other's wits. In the last game, Hinaikamālama challenges ʻAiwohikūpu to a friendly wager. If ʻAiwohikūpua wins, he can name his prize, but if Hinaikamālama wins, ʻAiwohikūpua must marry her. ʻAiwohikūpua agrees and makes every effort to win.

Hinaikamālama wins the game, and she immediately claims her prize. She wants to marry ʻAiwohikūpua as soon as possible.

ʻAiwohikūpua tells her that he first must go home and make plans for a wedding feast suitable enough for a woman as beautiful as Hinaikamālama, but he has no intention of marrying her. Instead, he makes a hasty retreat to the island of Hawaiʻi, where he chances upon the stunning Poliʻahu.

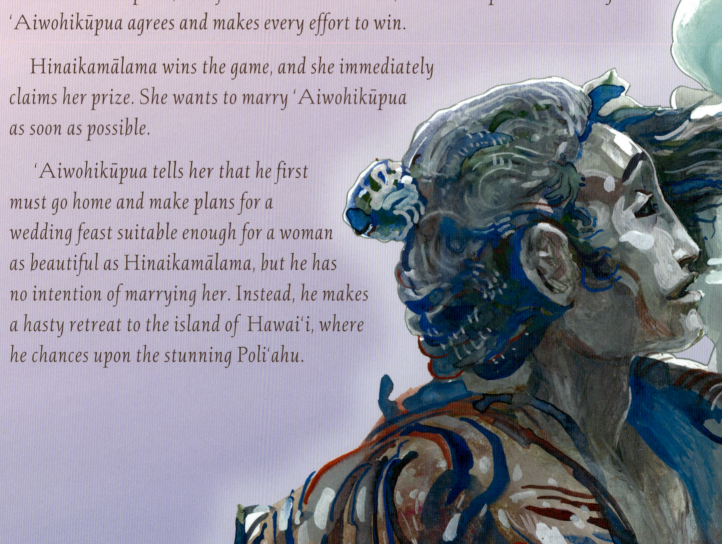

Poli'ahu is so lovely that 'Aiwohikūpua forgets all about Hinaikamālama. He wins her affection and asks her to come with him to his home in Kaua'i. Poli'ahu agrees and together they leave for Kaua'i to get married.

A magnificent wedding feast is planned. Every delicacy from the land and the ocean is prepared, and Poli'ahu and 'Aiwohikūpua are radiant in their love.

But their celebration is unexpectedly interrupted when an angry Hinaikamālama arrives at the wedding feast. She has come to claim the love that she had rightfully won playing kōnane. 'Aiwohikūpua has no choice but to honor the agreement that he had made with Hinaikamālama. He leaves Poli'ahu to join his rightful wife, and Hinaikamālama embraces and kisses him in front of Poli'ahu.

Poli'ahu is furious. She uses her godly powers to envelop the two lovers, first with intense heat and then with intense cold, until 'Aiwohikūpua and Hinaikamālama cannot tolerate it. The power of Poli'ahu forces them to separate forever.

Lilinoe, Waiau, & Kahoupokāne

Lilinoe, Waiau, and Kahoupokāne are sister of Poli'ahu. They are goddesses of extreme cold. The four sisters travel together often.

Lilinoe is the goddess of the mists and her shroud of fine rain can be seen on the mountaintops. Lilinoe is known as both the goddess of Haleakalā on the island of Maui and the goddess of Mauna Kea on the island of Hawai'i. She possesses the ability to restrain volcanic eruptions, extinguish fires, and reverse desolation. Waiau also lives on Mauna Kea on the island of Hawai'i. She has given her name to Waiau Lake, a cold pond of water located in a cinder cone. Kahoupokāne lives on Mount Hualālai on the island of Hawai'i.

Together the sisters are formidable, and even Pelehonuamea, the goddess of fire who has always been jealous of her sisters, is no match for them.

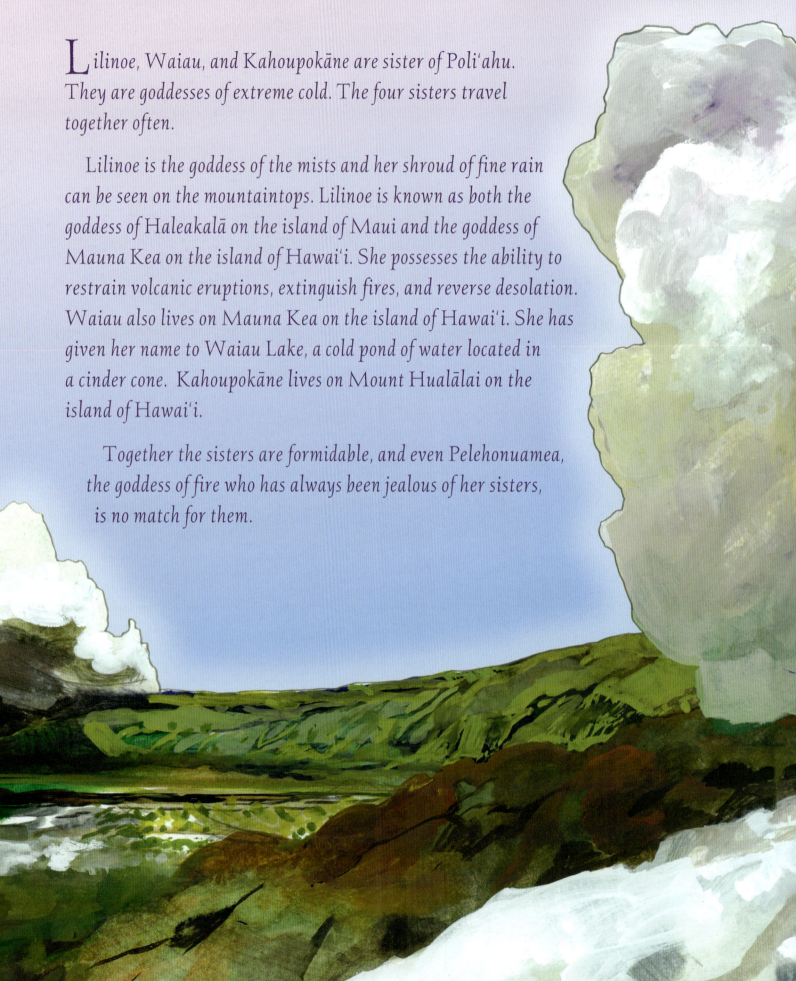

When Poliʻahu and her sisters visit the south slopes of Hāmākua on the island of Hawaiʻi for hill sledding, a stranger of unsurpassed beauty suddenly arrives before them. Poliʻahu and her sisters greet this beautiful stranger and then ask her to sled with them.

Poliʻahu and her sisters are surprised when they suddenly feel heat emanating from the earth. When the heat intensifies, Poliʻahu realizes the beautiful stranger is Pelehonuamea. Pelehonuamea casts off her disguise and commands scorching flames to burst forth from Kīlauea.

Poliʻahu and her sisters flee, but Pelehonuamea burns their cold capes anyway, so Poliʻahu turns back and casts a snowy covering over the mountain.

Earthquakes wrack the entire island in a battle between fire and snow. Poliʻahu gathers clouds heavy with snow and conjures up a blizzard that smothers the fires of Pelehonuamea, who retreats angrily to Kīlauea.

There are many such battles between Pelehonuamea and Poliʻahu. Pelehonuamea returns time after time to heave fiery hot lava onto the snowy mantle of Poliʻahu and her sisters, but Pelehonuamea is always beaten back. To this day, the mountain summit that Poliʻahu calls home is still frequently covered with snow.

Keaomelemele

Keaomelemele is the daughter of Hina and Kū, and is raised in Nuʻumealani by her ancestress Moʻoinanea, the great moʻo.

When Keaomelemele is about to be born, a spot of blood appears on the crown of her sleeping mother's head. Moʻoinanea takes this blood and wipes it on Kealohilani, a star that rises on the night of Mauli in the month of Welo. As Kealohilani rises, the blood is smeared across the sky, and Keaomelemele is born.

After Moʻoinanea names the infant Keaomelemele, she takes the child to her home in Kealohilani to be raised without the possibility of defilement. Moʻoinanea invokes the many varieties of clouds to act as guardians to Keaomelemele.

Readers of signs and omens worship Keaomelemele whose body form is the yellow cloud. She teaches priests to scan the stars and clouds for omens.

Keaomelemele, with her sisters Paliʻuli, Hiʻilaniwai, Maluaka, and Maunahina, become the first celebrated hula dancers and chanters from the Kauaʻi tradition of worship. After a ceremony to honor her accomplishments in hula, she chants. Her voice is so powerful, it splits apart Kōnāhuanui and Waolani to form Nuʻuanu.

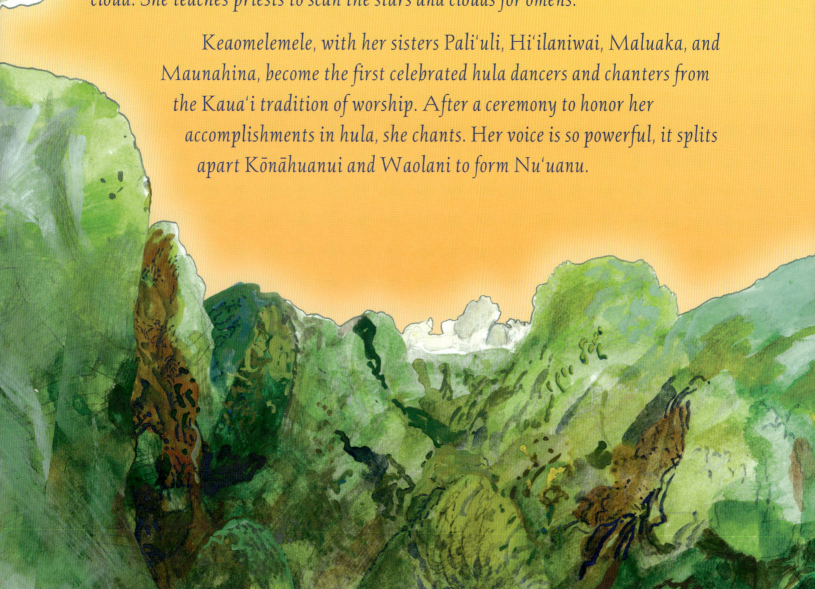

Moʻoinanea

Moʻoinanea is the most powerful moʻo, a supernatural being able to change her shape at will. Moʻoinanea is from the land of gods, Kuaihelani. She possesses two powerful trees, Makalei and Makuʻukao. These trees are able to produce unlimited amounts of vegetables, food, and fish.

When Keaomelemele, the granddaughter of Moʻoinanea, is about to be married, she invites Moʻoinanea to leave Kuaihelani and attend the wedding on the island of Oʻahu. Because Moʻoinanea possesses great mana, she decides that all of her relatives must attend Keaomelemele's wedding. She commands all the moʻo who live in Kuaihelani to swiftly prepare for the journey to Hawaiʻi. As the moʻo board the canoes, Moʻoinanea tells them that they will never return, but then promises them positions of power. All the moʻo obey because they have the utmost respect for Moʻoinanea and to defy this most powerful moʻo would result in instant death.

Moʻoinanea gives all of her powers to Wewehilani, the only moʻo allowed to remain in Kuaihelani. Wewehilani covers the islands with rain clouds and darkness, ensuring the protection of Kuaihelani forever.

Because so many moʻo disembark on to Oʻahu, when the first moʻo reaches Kapūkaki, the last of the moʻo are still in Waialua.

Many places in Hawaiʻi still bear the names of these moʻo who followed their great ancestress, Moʻoinanea, to Hawaiʻi. These moʻo give their names and become the guardians to freshwater streams, lakes, fishponds, rivers, and large pools of water.

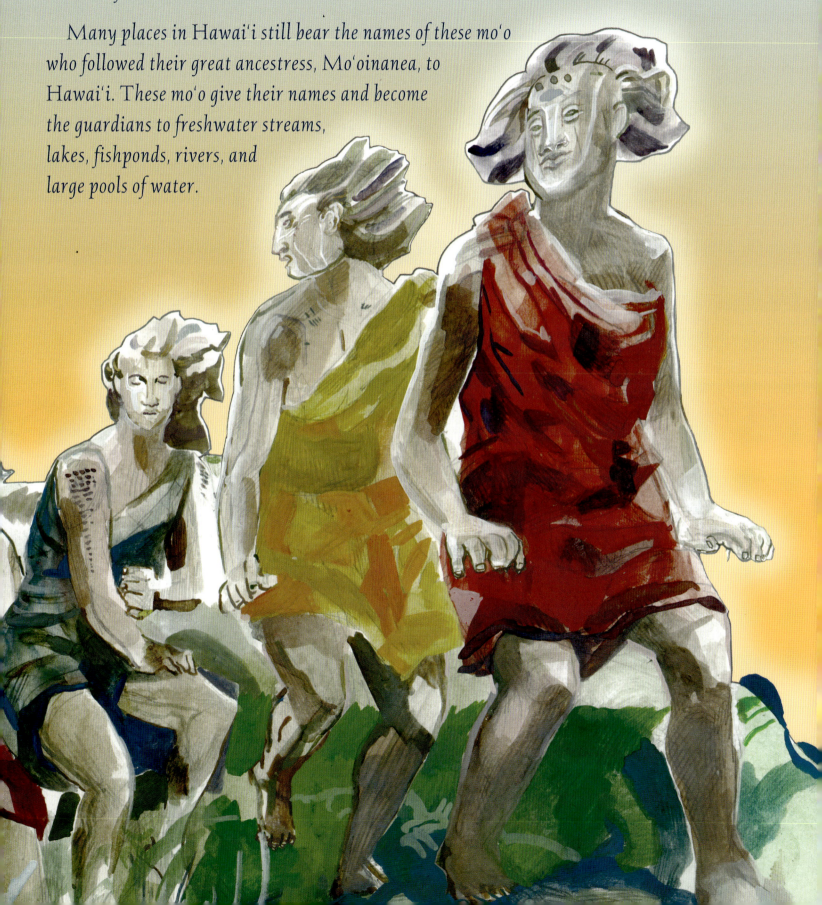

Kū'ulakai & Hinapukui'a

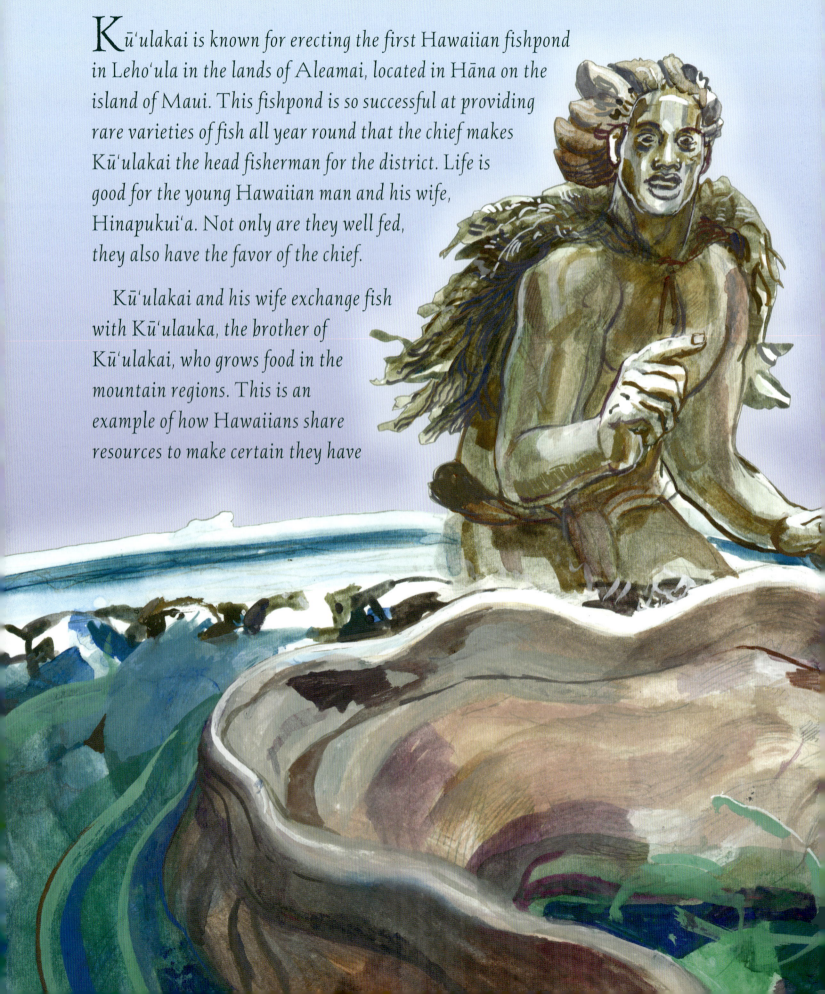

Kū'ulakai is known for erecting the first Hawaiian fishpond in Leho'ula in the lands of Aleamai, located in Hāna on the island of Maui. This fishpond is so successful at providing rare varieties of fish all year round that the chief makes Kū'ulakai the head fisherman for the district. Life is good for the young Hawaiian man and his wife, Hinapukui'a. Not only are they well fed, they also have the favor of the chief.

Kū'ulakai and his wife exchange fish with Kū'ulauka, the brother of Kū'ulakai, who grows food in the mountain regions. This is an example of how Hawaiians share resources to make certain they have what they need to survive: Those who live in the mountains exchange their harvest with those who live near the sea. Life gets even better for Kūʻulakai when his wife gives birth to their first child who they name ʻAiʻaiakūʻulakai.

One day Kūʻulakai notices that the number of fish in his pond is decreasing. This angers Kūʻulakai, and he is certain someone is stealing his fish.

One morning he sees a large eel slither through the sluice gates and is convinced that this eel is the thief stealing his fish. This eel, however, is none other than Koʻona, a powerful family guardian who protects the people of Wailau on the island of Molokaʻi. When Kūʻulakai considers how he will kill the eel, his wife advises him to have ʻAiʻaiakūʻulakai

ʻAiʻaiakūʻulakai captures the eel with the use of the powerful, magical fishhook, Mānaiakalani. The head of the eel is burned in an underground oven, but the eel's jaw and backbone turn into stone, which can still be seen in Hāna today. Everyone recognizes the power and expertise of ʻAiʻaiakūʻulakai.

The eel spirit of Koʻona travels back to Molokaʻi and appears in a dream to its keeper, who swiftly journeys to Hāna to avenge the death of his beloved guardian. After the eel's keeper arrives in Hāna, he becomes the chief's servant, but only to gain the chief's trust so that he may plot his revenge.

One day the eel's keeper goes to Kūʻulakai on behalf of the chief to ask for fish, which Kūʻulakai gives him willingly. As he gives the fish to the eel's keeper, Kūʻulakai tells him to tell the chief to preserve the fish by cutting it up and salting it.

But when the eel's keeper presents the fish to the chief, he lies. The keeper tells the chief that Kūʻulakai said his head should be cut up and his body should be salted like the fish. The chief is insulted.

The chief commands all of his people to hunt down Kūʻulakai and burn him alive, but most of the people of Aleamai love Kūʻulakai and refuse to obey the chief. Kūʻulakai has always freely given fish to whoever needed food. But there were also those who lived in Hāna who were never touched by the generosity of Kūʻulakai, or those who did not want to incur the wrath of the chief. These people surround the house of Kūʻulakai and Hinapukuiʻa with wood and burn it down.

Kūʻulakai knows who is responsible for causing his family such anguish, and he orders ʻAiʻaiakūʻulakai to kill anyone who has tried to kill him. Kūʻulakai gives ʻAiʻaiakūʻulakai all of his knowledge as well as instructions on how to escape. Kūʻulakai also gives his son his most important possessions – Mānaiakalani, his great fishhook; Kahuoi, his pearl fishhook for catching bonito; Lehoʻula, his red cowry for catching octopus; and Kūʻulaauakūʻulakai, a stone that creates all the fish in the sea.

The guards of the chief enter into the house and bind the hands of Kūʻulakai, Hinapukuiʻa, and ʻAiʻaiakūʻulakai. The three are tied to posts and their house is set on fire. As soon as the fire is lit, the cords binding their hands magically loosen and fall. Kūʻulakai and Hinapukuiʻa look lovingly at their son as their spirits leave their bodies and fly out over the ocean, taking every single fish and sea creature with them.

As huge flames engulf the house, ʻAiʻaiakūʻulakai calls out his father's name to punish those who have wronged him. Waves of flames spew out of the house and selectively burn those responsible for setting the house on fire. The keeper of the eel, Koʻona, is burned to death. ʻAiʻaiakūʻulakai walks calmly out of the burning house, and as instructed by his father, heads towards a cave near Kaʻiwiopele.

The village of Aleamai is also punished, as there is not a single fish left in the ocean. They call upon the name of Kūʻulakai for favor in fishing, for he is now a god.

ʻAiʻaikūʻulakai

ʻAiʻaiakūʻulakai pities the people of Aleamai. Since the death of his parents, every single fish has left the ocean, and the people are in great need of fish. ʻAiʻaiakūʻulakai erects the first fishing shrine in Lehoʻula with Kūʻulaauakūʻulakai, the small stone that creates fish, given to him by his father.

ʻAiʻaiakūʻulakai takes the stone god Pōhakumūone, faces it towards the fishpond that was built by his father, and offers a prayer to his father and mother.

ʻAiʻaiakūʻulakai teaches his friend Pilihāwāwā how to pray to the fishing shrine for favor in fishing. He instructs Pilihāwāwā to offer the first catch to Kūʻulakai and Hinapukuiʻa, for if there should be any mistake or offense, his parents might refuse favor and once again there would be no fish.

As soon as the proper protocols are observed, the fish return in great numbers. One of the villagers takes a fresh catch of wrasse to the chief. The chief slips the fish into his mouth, but it gets stuck in his throat and he dies, and the revenge for the death of Kūʻulakai and Hinapukuiʻa is complete.

ʻAiʻaiakūʻulakai establishes fishing shrines throughout the island of Maui, and he gives the guardianship of each of these shrines to a local resident. ʻAiʻaiakūʻulakai teaches these guardians the prayers, along with how to call upon the names of his parents and make the proper offerings.

'Ai'aiakū'ulakai then travels to each of the islands to build more fishing shrines. On the island of Lāna'i, he carves symbols onto a rock and places it into the water. When he begins his prayers to his parents, the rock stirs and then crawls into the ocean. And then, as soon as 'Ai'aiakū'ulakai finishes his prayers, the rock reappears and crawls back to him. 'Ai'aiakū'ulakai moves closer to the rock and discovers that it has turned into a turtle. To this day, the turtle will enter into the sea and return to shore to lay its eggs. 'Ai'aiakū'ulakai names this beach on the island of Lāna'i, Polihua.

Sometimes the fishing shrine is used to attract a certain variety of fish. For instance, Mālei, the fishing shrine in Makapu'u on the island of O'ahu, is specifically used to attract parrotfish.

'Ai'aiakū'ulakai honors the name of his parents by building important fishing shrines all over Hawai'i. He also teaches the Hawaiian people a valuable lesson: In order to be successful in any endeavor, it is important to follow the proper protocols.

Sources

Versions of the stories contained in this book can be found in the following texts, audio tapes, and manuscripts.

Andrews, Lorrin. *Dictionary of the Hawaiian Language.*
    Hong Kong: Island Heritage Publishing, 2003.

Beckwith, Martha. *Hawaiian Mythology.*
    Honolulu: University of Hawai'i Press, 1970.

Fornander, Abraham. *Ancient History of the Hawaiian People to the Times of Kamehameha I.* Vol. II.
    Honolulu: Mutual Publishing, 1996.

———. *Fornander Collection of Hawaiian Antiquities and Folk-lore* (3 vols.).
    Memoirs of the Bernice Pauahi Bishop Museum, Vol. 4, 5, 6.
    Honolulu: Bishop Museum Press, 1916-1917.

Gutmanis, June. *Nā Pule Kahiko: Ancient Hawaiian Prayers.* Honolulu: Editions Limited, 1983.

Haole, C. J. "A Prayer to Hapuu." *Hawaiian Ethnological Notes.* 1895. Vol. 1: 251.

Ii, John Papa. *Fragments of Hawaiian History.* Honolulu: Bishop Museum Press, 1959.

Kamakau, Samuel M. "Ke Mele Na Kaleiopaoa i Kilauea." Unpublished manuscript.
    Honolulu: Bishop Museum Archives.

———. *Tales and Traditions of the People of Old: Na Mo'olelo a ka Po'e Kahiko.*
    Translated by Mary Kawena Pukui. Honolulu: Bishop Museum Press, 1993.

Kame'eleihiwa, Lilikalā. *A Legendary Tradition of Kamapua'a, The Hawaiian Pig God.*
    Honolulu: Bishop Museum Press, 1996.

"Ka Moolelo o Kepakailiula." *Ka Nupepa Kuokoa.* February 2, 1865. Book 4, Number 5.

"Ka Moolelo no Pele – Kona Hana, Kona Mana, a me Kona Noho Ana." *Ka Nupepa Kuokoa.*
    February 2, 1865. Book 4, Number 5.

Keaulumoku. *The Kumulipo: An Hawaiian Creation Myth.* Liliuokalani, trans. Kentfield, California: Pueo Press, 1978.

Keonehaliokalani, George M. "Mookuauhau o Akahikapomanomano." Unpublished manuscript.
    Honolulu: Bishop Museum Archives.

———. "He Moolelo no Hawaii Lani Honua." Unpublished manuscript. Honolulu: Bishop Museum Archives.

Kepelino, Keauokalani. *Kepelino's Traditions of Hawaii.* Translated and edited by Martha Warren Beckwith.
    Honolulu: Bishop Museum Press, 1932.

Kuamuamu. "Kealiikauaokau." Unpublished manuscript. Honolulu: Bishop Museum Archives.

Kuhi, P. K. "O Ke Kaua a Pele i Kahiki." Unpublished manuscript. Honolulu: Bishop Museum Archives.

Lono, Mahealani, and others. Conversation recorded on August 22, 1960. Kawaihae, Hawai'i.

Malo, David. *Hawaiian Antiquities.* Translated by Nathaniel Emerson. Honolulu: Bishop Museum Press, 1976.

Marciel, Josephine, and others. Conversation recorded on November 30, 1961. Kaupō, Maui.

Moses, Manu. "He Kaao o Keaomelemele." *Ka Nupepa Kuokoa.* September 20, 1884. Volume 23, Number 38.

———. "Ka Moolelo o Kihapiilani." *Ka Nupepa Kuokoa.* February 23, 1884. Book 23, Number 8.

———. "Ka Moolelo o Ninauapoe." *Ka Nupepa Kuokoa.* February 23, 1884. Book 23, Number 8.

Nakuina, Emma M. et al. *Nanaue the Sharkman and Other Hawaiian Shark Stories.* Honolulu: Kalamakū Press, 1994.

Nakuina, Moses. *The Wind Gourd of La'amaomao.* Translated by Esther T. Mookini and Sarah Nakoa.
    Honolulu: Kalamakū Press, 1992.

"O Wakea, O Kahikoluamea/O Papa, o Papahanaumoku." *Ka Na'i Aupuni.* June 21, 1906.

Paikulu. "He Mele no Lohiau." Unpublished chant. Honolulu: Bishop Museum Archives.

———. "O Laniuli Wahine Akua o Nuumealani/O Kamehanalani, o Kamehaikana." Unpublished chant.
    Honolulu: Bishop Museum Archives.

Paele. "O Laniuli Wahine Akua o Nuumealani/O Kamehanalani, o Kamehaikana." *Mele Manuscript Collection of Helen Roberts.*
    Honolulu: Bishop Museum Archives.

Poepoe, Joseph M. "Genealogy of Haumea." Unpublished manuscript. Honolulu: Bishop Museum Archives.

———. "Hoomaka ana o ka Lahui o Hawaii Nei." Unpublished manuscript. Honolulu: Bishop Museum Archives.

———. "Moolelo Hawaii Kahiko." *Ka Na'i Aupuni.* June 21, 1906. Book 3, Number 17.

———. "Ka Moolelo Kaao o Hiiaka-I-ka-Poli-o-Pele." *Kuokoa Home Rula.* January 10, 1908.

Pukui, Mary Kawena, and Samuel Elbert. *Hawaiian Dictionary.* Honolulu: University of Hawai'i Press, 1986.

Rice, William Hyde. "No Pele a me Kona Kaikaina, Hiiaka i ka Poli o Pele." *Ka Hoku o Hawaii.* May 21, 1908. Book 3, Number 4.